Laos

by Adam Markovics

Consultant: Marjorie Faulstich Orellana, PhD
Professor of Urban Schooling
University of California, Los Angeles

BEARPORT PUBLISHING

New York, New York

Credits

Cover, © Patchra Suttivirat/Shutterstock and © Sirikornt/iStock; TOC, © 501room/Shutterstock; 4, © MAGNIFIER/Shutterstock; 5T, © backpacker79/Shutterstock; 5B, © saravutpics/Shutterstock; 7, © Santiti Chanpeng/Shutterstock; 8, © Kantarote/iStock; 9, © 9comeback/Shutterstock; 10T, © taratipman/Shutterstock; 10BL, © Matt Gibson/Shutterstock; 10BR, © Somchai Siriwanarangson/Shutterstock; 11, © Petra Christen/Shutterstock; 12, © Godong/Alamy; 13, © Neil McAllister/Alamy; 14, © Khoroshunova Olga/Shutterstock; 15T, © Chaoborus/CC BY-SA 4.0; 15B, © Alistair Laming/Alamy; 16, © Bridgeman Images; 17T, © Stefan Auth/imageBROKER/AGE Fotostock; 17B, © Olga Kolos/Alamy; 18L, © Andrii Lutsyk/Shutterstock; 18–19, © amnat30/Shutterstock; 20T, © David Noton Photography/Alamy; 20B, © Lmspencer/Shutterstock; 21, © Sean Sprague/Alamy; 22L, © Kris Tan/Shutterstock; 22–23, © Simonkolton/iStock; 23R, © Mr. Black/Shutterstock; 24, © Tanawat Palee/Shutterstock; 25, © Fredrik von Erichsen/picture-alliance/Newscom; 26T, © Phoutthavong SOUVANNACHAK/Shutterstock; 26B, © MR. Sitthipong Moonlasri/Shutterstock; 27, © aluxum/iStock; 28L, © DEGAS Jean-Pierre/Hemis/AGE Fotostock; 28–29, © Urs Flueeler/Zoonar/AGE Fotostock; 30T, © Oleg_Mit/Shutterstock and © Henning Marquardt/Shutterstock; 30B, © Latte Art/Shutterstock; 31 (T to B), © Michael Luhrenberg/iStock, © John Bill/Shutterstock, © okili77/Shutterstock, © Stefan Auth/imageBROKER/Alamy, © southtownboy/iStock, and © Guy Chaiyapruk/Shutterstock; 32, © Boris15/Shutterstock.

Publisher: Kenn Goin
Senior Editor: Joyce Tavolacci
Creative Director: Spencer Brinker
Design: Debrah Kaiser
Photo Researcher: Thomas Persano

Library of Congress Cataloging-in-Publication Data

Names: Markovics, Adam, author.
Title: Laos / by Adam Markovics.
Description: New York, N.Y. : Bearport Publishing, 2019. | Series: Countries
  we come from | Includes bibliographical references and index.
Identifiers: LCCN 2018009292 (print) | LCCN 2018010082 (ebook) |
ISBN 9781684027385 (ebook) | ISBN 9781684026920 (library)
Subjects: LCSH: Laos—Juvenile literature.
Classification: LCC DS555.3 (ebook) | LCC DS555.3 .M38 2019 (print) |
DDC 959.4—dc23
LC record available at https://lccn.loc.gov/2018009292

For more information, write to Bearport Publishing Company, Inc., 45 West 21st Street, Suite 3B, New York, New York 10010. Printed in the United States of America.

10 9 8 7 6 5 4 3 2 1

Contents

This Is Laos

Tropical

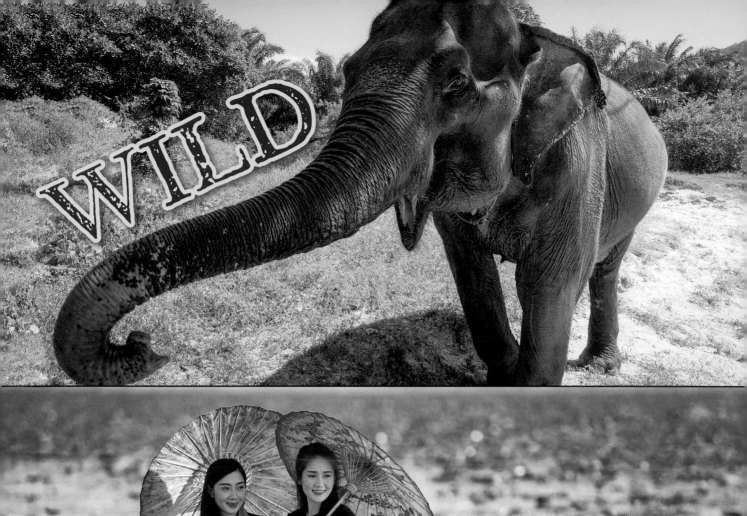

WILD

Full of Wonder

Laos (LOUS) is a country in Southeast Asia.

Over 7 million people live there.

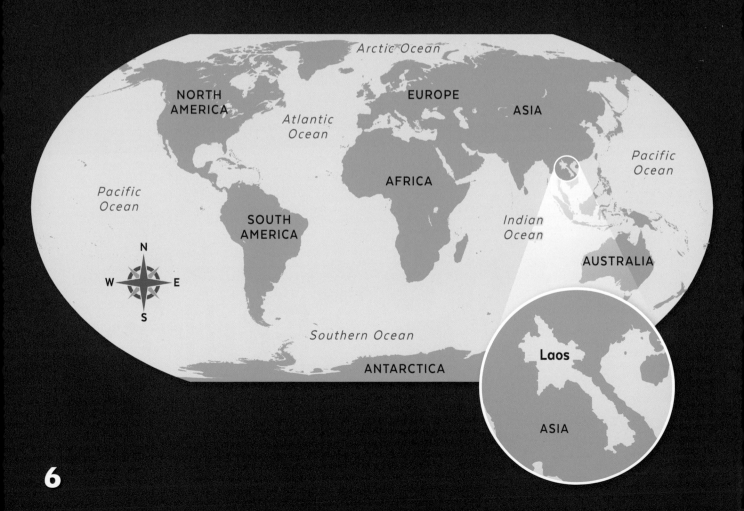

People from Laos
are called Laotians.

Tall mountains and thick forests cover Laos.

The highest mountain is over 9,000 feet (2,743 m) tall!

Laos's **climate** is warm and damp.

Many rivers also twist through Laos.

Mekong River

Uncommon creatures live in Laos.

Giant catfish swim in the country's rivers.

Clouded leopards and moon bears prowl the forests.

giant catfish

clouded leopard

moon bear

Thousands of Asian elephants once lived in Laos. Today, only about 500 remain.

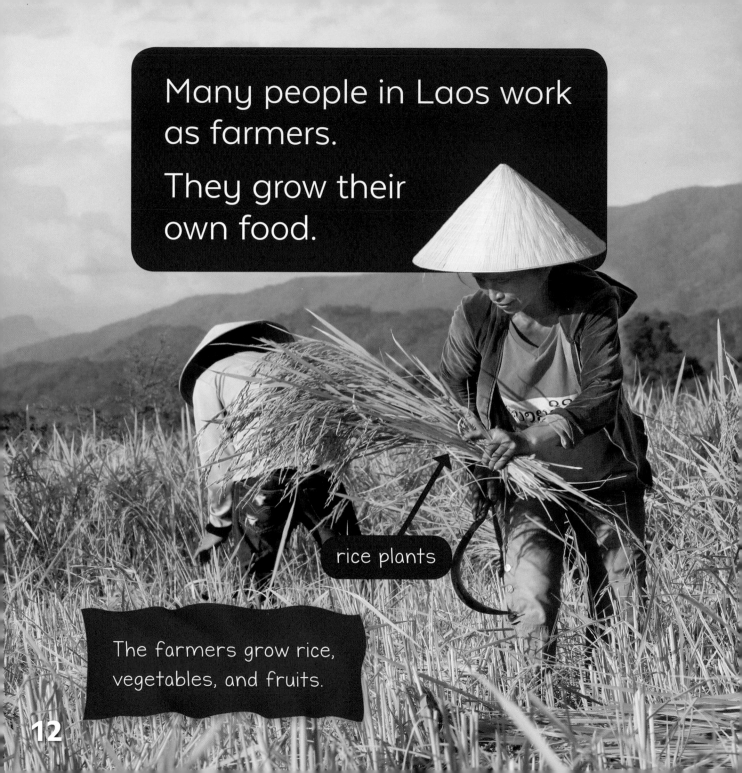

Many people in Laos work as farmers.

They grow their own food.

rice plants

The farmers grow rice, vegetables, and fruits.

Often, farmers live in small wooden houses with their families.

a farmhouse in Laos

Laos has a long, rich history.
People first settled there
around 10,000 years ago.

2,000-year-old
stone carvings

In 1353, a man named Fa Ngum (FAH NUHM) became king of Laos.

He called the land Lan Xang (LAN SANG).

Fa Ngum

Lan Xang means "kingdom of a million elephants."

In 1779, people from Thailand took control of Laos.

Then, French settlers came to power in 1893.

French settlers

In 1953, Laos became an **independent** country.

Today, **communist** leaders rule Laos.

17

Laos has a handful of big cities.

The **capital** is Vientiane, or Viangchan.

It has many busy outdoor markets.

About 210,000 people live in Vientiane.

19

Lao is the main language of Laos.

This is how you say *hello*:

ສະບາຍດີ
(sa-BAI-dee)

Lao script

ແໜ່ງທ່ອງທ່ຽວ ທຳມະຊາດ
ອຸທິຍານ ນ້ຳຕົກຕາດກວາງຊີ
Kouang Si Waterfall

Lao is written
in Lao script.

20

This is how you say *good luck*:

ໂຊກດີ (SOK-DEE)

a woman selling birds for good luck

Laotian food is fresh and tasty.

Sticky rice is a favorite dish.

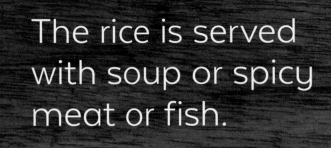

The rice is served with soup or spicy meat or fish.

Some Laotian drinks are served in a plastic bag. Just stick in a straw and enjoy!

What sports are popular in Laos?

People love kataw (ka-TOW).

It's like volleyball, but players can't use their hands.

Instead, they only kick the ball!

Laotians also enjoy beetle wrestling! They put two beetles together to see which one is stronger.

Most people in Laos are Buddhist.

They **worship** in temples or shrines.

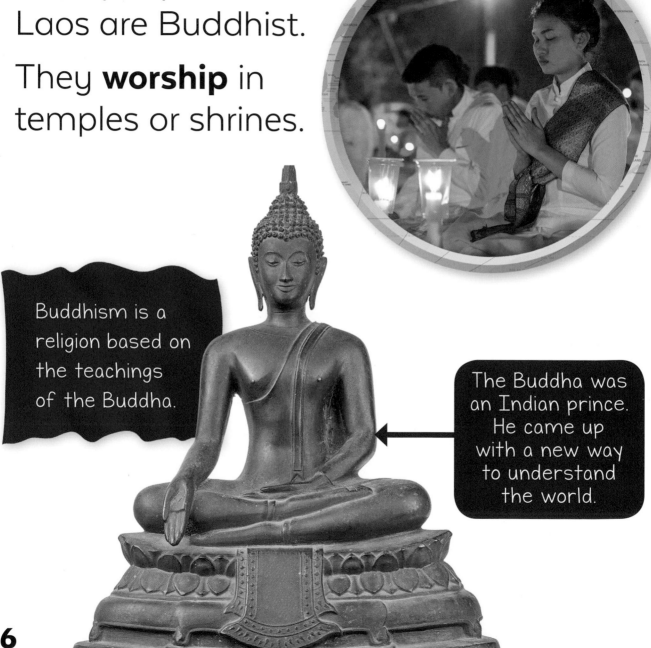

Buddhism is a religion based on the teachings of the Buddha.

The Buddha was an Indian prince. He came up with a new way to understand the world.

Many Laotian men live as Buddhist **monks**. They wear bright orange robes.

27

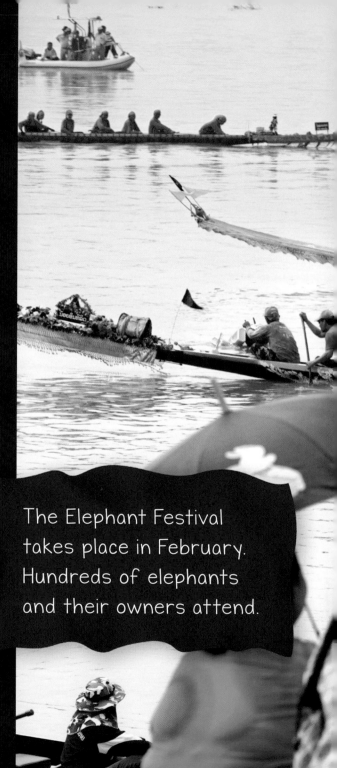

The Boat Racing Festival is held every October.

Long boats zip along the Mekong River.

Racers paddle with all their might.

The Elephant Festival takes place in February. Hundreds of elephants and their owners attend.

Who will win?

Fast Facts

Capital city:
Vientiane (Viangchan)

Population of Laos:
Over 7 million

Main language: Lao

Money: Kip

Major religion: Buddhism

Neighboring countries include: China, Vietnam, Thailand, Myanmar (Burma), and Cambodia

Cool Fact: Laos is home to Southeast Asia's largest waterfall. It's bigger than Niagara Falls!

Glossary

capital (KAP-uh-tuhl) a city where a country's government is based

climate (KLYE-mit) the typical weather in a place

communist (COM-yuh-nist) a person who supports a system in which all goods and property are shared

independent (in-duh-PEN-duhnt) free of control from others

monks (MUHNGKS) religious people who have devoted their lives to prayer and teaching

worship (WUR-ship) to adore and honor something or someone

Index

Read More

Epstein, Steven Jay. *Lao Folktales.* Chiang Mai, Thailand: Silkworm Books (2006).

Oachs, Emily Rose. *Laos (Blastoff Readers).* Minnetonka, MN: Bellwether Media (2016).

Learn More Online

To learn more about Laos, visit
www.bearportpublishing.com/CountriesWeComeFrom

About the Author

Adam Markovics lives in Ossining, New York. He has a pet rabbit named Pearl who enjoys sitting next to him as he writes.